By Bι
to Chris

Candlestick Press

Published by:

Candlestick Press,

Diversity House, 72 Nottingham Road, Arnold, Nottingham UK NG5 6LF

www.candlestickpress.co.uk

Design and typesetting by Craig Twigg

Printed by Ratcliff & Roper Print Group, Nottinghamshire, UK

ISBN 978 1 913627 00 3

Contents

Introduction

What a quiet joy it has been to make these Christmas poems for you and Candlestick Press. Most were written during the beautiful sunshine of Spring 2020, a time that will always be associated with the coronavirus. Lockdown brought changes to North County Dublin: the Olive café and the headland in Skerries were off limits, so I wrote in the shelter of the harbour wall as boats and seabirds came and went with the morning tide.

I discovered this was a friendly place to imagine all things Christmas. For a child Christmas is like a big red ship, lit up with stars, fairy lights and candles, sailing into harbour through winter's darkness. It makes magic and strangeness normal. Christmas Eve fills the child's imagination to overflowing; is it any wonder poets have always been attracted to its light?

Strangely enough, the poem that first lit up poetry for me was a Christmas one: 'Stopping by Woods on a Snowy Evening'. In a grey classroom in Dublin, on a wintry Friday afternoon, Brother Kelly wrote Frost's enchanting lines on the blackboard, word by chalky word. I was lost in snowy woods with the man and his horse, my eyes following Brother Kelly's hand until: "And miles to go before I sleep, And miles to go before I sleep". Its ending was so like a prayer, I almost said "Amen".

Brother Kelly saw everyone busily scribbling except me. "Not writing, Curtis. How are you supposed to do your homework?" I told him I'd already learnt it by heart and was ordered to prove it. I stood up and a river of snowy words poured out. It was as if a 1000 watt bulb had lit up inside me. I knew from that moment what I was put on this earth to do.

Tony Curtis

The Angel's Promise

It is the edge of winter.
An old storyteller
is coming in from the cold
at the end of a long journey.
A year in the making,
it began with fireworks
and is ending in candlelight.
She has only one story left:
The Angel's Promise.
It is an old Roman tale.
It involves a star, a birth,
and an enchanted promise.
Its words, a blessing on us all,
though, in truth, it is a tale made
for children listening at the stable door.

Evergreen

My hands, my coat, my knees
were cold and wet from climbing
through the sprawling holly tree.

In the kitchen, before my brother
and I set out, our mother gave us
the fruits of her country upbringing:

Now boys,
it was a beautiful summer
with lots of birds and bees
in and out of the leaves,
so there are bound to be
necklaces of berries woven
into the branches of holly trees.
Make sure to bring some home.
Your father's mother will complain
if there are not red berries
on the holly sprays.
You'd think she was a blackbird.

So on I climbed higher
and deeper into the holly tree
with not a red berry to be seen.

Below me
on the grass
my brother began to sing –

a small,
lonely choir
on this side of the mountain.

His beautiful
soprano voice
soft and sweet and true

The Holly and the Ivy,
an *elfin* spell
enchanting the tree.

And suddenly,
there they were, berries,
glowing red as Rudolph's nose.

Christmas Joy

Nobody is old at this time of the year.

It softly fell from the winter sky,
    fell over
the rooftops and the river,
    fell so quietly
even the sleepy dreamer,
    our smallest child,
hardly felt it settling in the air,
    she just stirred
a little under the covers,
    then went on dreaming
winter frost and reindeer
    footprints in the snow.

The Winter Moon

The Earth's old lantern
glimmering above the river
the woods and the town.

Who holds it high?
What ancient soul
listening at our door

this Solstice night
whispers to the sun
bring back the light?

The Darkest Evening

This Solstice night
a bell tolls along
the edge of the valley,
children are singing
carols in the church.

Their sweet voices
sing through
blue eyes,
green eyes,
brown eyes.

This winter harmony,
clear as a mountain stream,
echoes through the dark,
through church
and graveyard,

filling the night
with hallelujah,
gloria,
with holly and ivy,
and *Good King Wenceslas.*

It soars
over the valley
like a glorious raven
calling back
the light.

The Attic Room

There were long fingers
of ice on the gate
this morning
as if a ghost had touched it.

That was Henry,
he was probably
going home to bed,
my son said.

He's old, like you.
He gets tired walking
the house all night
sighing and singing.

So, this Henry sighs and sings?
Oh yes, Henry loves to sing,
and at this time of the year
he loves singing carols.

He has a sweet
voice, like me.
He was in a choir too
when he was my age.

Last night he sang
"Jingle Bells"
all through the night.
Henry loves "Jingle Bells".

But he says he hates
the six flights of stairs
to the attic in this creaky
old house of ours.

In fact, he says he is
a little frightened of the dark
and he hates the cold nights –
"Jingle Bells" *lifts his spirits.*

He usually leaves by
the back door and meets
Milly, she's lovely.
She is the ghost from next door.

She's been wearing
a red Santa hat
for the last month.
Milly loves Christmas.

She is older than Henry.
She died in 1882,
a year before
Henry was born

in this house,
in this room.
That's why Henry
is so fond of me.

She must have been
busy this morning
if Henry left
through the front door.

Where did you say Henry
was going?
Home, my son said.
Home? Where's home?

The old cemetery
in Harold's Cross.
Harold's Cross?
That's miles away!

Yes, my son said,
that is why
he catches
the early bus.

All the ghosts do.
Henry says he can never
get a seat, and the conductor
is a miserable old soul

who won't let anyone sing,
not even "Jingle Bells",
which is a great tune
to sing on a bus at Christmas.

By Bus to Christmas

This year I am going by bus to Christmas.
Last year I went by hippopotamus.
It was slow and grey
and kept losing its way.
So this year I am going by bus to Christmas.

My mother says to go in style
I should go by crocodile.
But though they have a lovely smile,
would you really trust a crocodile?
No! So this year I am going by bus to Christmas.

My brother Seamus, who loves his bed,
says I should go by elephant instead.
An elephant would be good in the snow,
but would an elephant know where to go?
No! So this year I am going by bus to Christmas.

The man from the zoo came to say
the elephant is free on Christmas Day.
Camel, giraffe, monkey, mouse,
I don't care what he brings to the house.
This year I am going by bus to Christmas.

My mother is going by plane.
My father is going by train.
My sister doesn't want to make a fuss,
so she is going by the slow hippopotamus.
But me, I am going by bus to Christmas.

And not an ordinary bus,
but a Christmas bus
with snow on the roof
and holly on the sides,
a magical bus that flies.

With stars for windows,
snowballs for wheels,
and an engine that sings
The Snowman's Song
  I'm walking in the air...

as it toots along.
And the driver must have
a nose that glows
so he knows
by snow-light where he goes.

And it is not very far I'm told,
just a snowy ride to the top of the world.
Under the bridges, over the clouds,
following a map of stars.
Yes, I am travelling by bus to Christmas.

And so are the reindeer,
and so are the elves,
and so are Santa and Mrs. Claus
and all and all and all because
it's best to go by bus to Christmas.

When Frida Kahlo came for Christmas

When Frida Kahlo came for Christmas
she helped decorate the house.
It looked magnificent with Mexican
greens and gold, and deep ruby reds.
The rooms were luminous, glimmering.

But she kept her best surprise for
Christmas Eve when she dressed
her husband, Diego, in a red Santa suit.
He had the build, the big round belly.

The children's eyes glistened to see him,
but Frida sat rigid on her chair, observing
the joy of small hands at Christmas.

As her eyes were painting childhood,
her long black hair was sweeping it away.

The Red-breasted Lookout on Christmas Eve

It is Christmas Eve sixty years ago.
I am five years old: a curious child
out in the cold, searching the night
sky for a glimpse of Santa's sleigh.

I turn and my father is at the shed
putting his bicycle away. Seeing me,
he asks if I have seen the big red man.
"No," I say, *"but I spotted a red robin."*

"Ah, the robin," my father says,
"the lookout. The robin always appears
before the reindeer. He is making sure
little boys are tucked up tight and dreaming."

Then he lifts me up into the air
and I hang there in the branches
of his arms like a red-cheeked robin
laughing my head off with fright.

Now my father is gone,
and every Christmas Eve
that childhood memory
lifts me into the air,

and in a sad heart shake,
the silver joy of Christmas
is everywhere, and everywhere
is Christmas once again.

Yeats at Stone Cottage

The village of Coleman's Hatch
in East Sussex remembers
the Irish poet W.B. Yeats.
In the winter of 1913
he came to live in *Stone Cottage,*
an L-shaped dwelling looking out
over Winnie the Pooh's *500 Acre Wood.*

They especially remember
the morning
he wandered the town
like a wayfarer,
muttering to himself,
pushing at doors,
looking through windows.

They had the story
from the housekeeper,
the marvellously named
Mrs. Welfare. Alice Welfare.
She cooked and cleaned,
ironed and polished,
kept him and his verses neat.

She said he got back
to the cottage early,
his hair white with frost,
his coat, his face, his boots
flecked with snow. Opening
the door he declared into the air,
as if to a cat or a shade:

I don't know what's going on,
it's like plague has struck the village.
There isn't a living soul to be seen.
The teashop has its curtains drawn.
The blacksmith's forge is dark.
Even the post office is closed.
How am I to get my letters off to London?

What can it be, Mrs. Welfare,
what can it be?
It's Christmas morning, Mr. Yeats, sir.
People are still a-bed.
It is always this hushed
until the church bells
crack the stillness.

Christmas, Mrs. Welfare?
Yes, sir, Christmas Day. Maybe you don't
have Christmas in Ireland,
what with your people
being so fond of the drink
and it best not to give them an excuse.
Oh no, Mrs. Welfare, the Irish love Christmas.

Well then sir, a Merry Christmas to you,
and as our Mr. Dickens has Tiny Tim say,
"God bless us, every one!"
Yes, indeed, God bless us all
on this peaceful Christmas morning.
Maybe you could put something
like it in one of your Christmas poems.

From under the Christmas Tree

You were five,
I was six
so I was in charge.
I said, we'd go when we heard
Santa's footsteps on the stairs.
You said, we'd go when it was bright,
but that was only because you were
young and afraid of the dark.
So we went with my plan
and crept down the stairs
when the house was still and whisper quiet.

Some of my presents were as big as you,
but what they were, I can't recall.
You got a doll that cried,
a blue tea set,
a book of fairy tales
and a jigsaw showing Santa's beardy face.

I remember
I spent hours making that puzzle.
Santa's red cheeks emerging before me
while you served lemonade tea
and crumbles of iced cake to your doll
and your new best friend, the silver fairy
who lived between the pages of your Christmas book
and slept in a straw bed like baby Jesus in his crib.

The Hushed House

Every Christmas
I wake early

to watch the snow
that doesn't fall;

to listen to the bells
that do not ring;

to hear the laughter
of children grown and gone.

I descend the stairs,
light the tree,

and move quietly
through the empty rooms

until I find you,
almost in darkness,

with the breakfast made
and laid out on a red table cloth

with holly and cards
and candles glowing,

your dishevelled smile
filled with Christmas light,

your dark eyes,
cheeky as a robin's,

settling my heart,
melting my winter weather.